Puddles Gets A New Home

Dedicated to our beloved pet guinea pig, Puddles

Written and Illustrated By:

Neva Capezza & Mary Alice Barrows

Once upon a time a little girl and a little guinea pig have their most cherished dream come true.

Anna peered out of her bedroom window and wished for a friend

The little guinea pig peered out of his cage in a pet shop and thought.... "Why can't I get a home like everyone else? I just want someone to love and care for me."

One evening after dinner, Anna's mother walked into her room, where she often played alone, to check on her and spend some time with her. She found Anna very sad. "What's wrong, Honey?" Anna replied, "Oh, mommy, I wish I had a brother or sister to play with because I feel so lonely sometimes."

Her mom comforted her and helped her to get ready for bed. Tomorrow was a school day and a work day for her and Anna's dad.

As she left the room, Anna's mom thought to herself: "Hmm, since I work all day and there is no one for her to play with, maybe she needs a 'little friend' to keep her company. I have an idea."

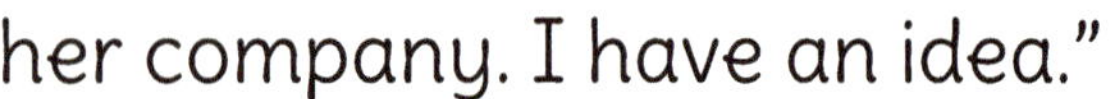

So, one day soon after, Anna's mother was able to leave work early and surprise Anna by picking her up from kindergarten. As they walked to the car, her mother said, "Anna guess what?"

"What, mommy, what? Anna asked excitedly. "I have a big surprise for you this afternoon." Her mother replied. "But first, let's have some lunch."

They had lunch at Anna's favorite restaurant, and she asked her mother over and over again what the big surprise was. Her mom said, "You will just have to wait and see, but I promise you that you will really love it." Anna was so excited.

Her mother stopped and parked the car right in front of a pet shop! Anna's eyes grew wide as she began to realize what the Big Surprise might be. Anna asked as they walked into the pet shop. "Mommy, why are we here? Are you and daddy going to let me get a pet? Oh! Please say yes." As she twirled round and round in her happiness.

"Yes, Anna, your Dad and I think it is time for you to have your first pet, but it can't be too big. It must be something that you can take care of and play with nicely."

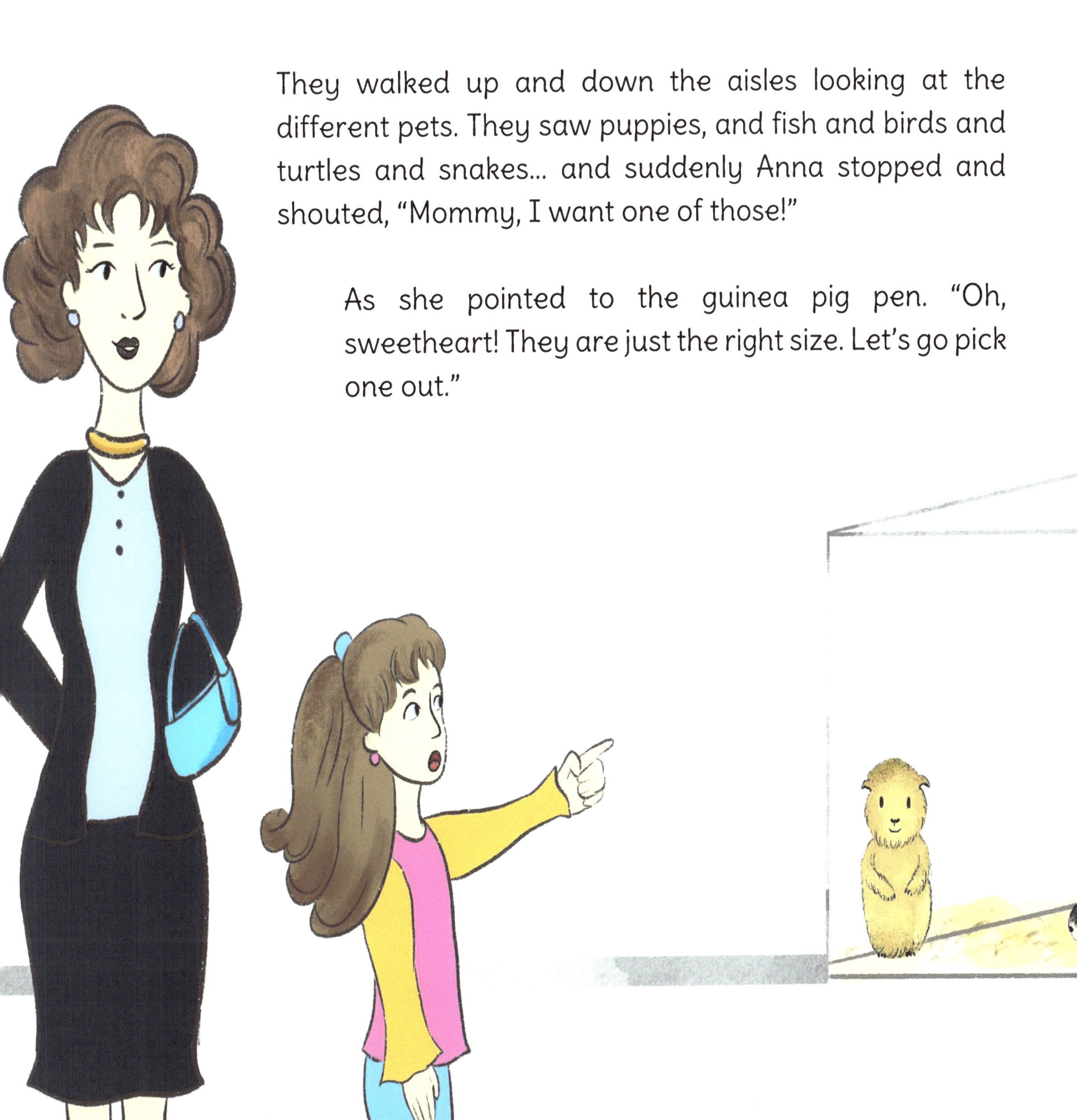

They walked up and down the aisles looking at the different pets. They saw puppies, and fish and birds and turtles and snakes... and suddenly Anna stopped and shouted, "Mommy, I want one of those!"

As she pointed to the guinea pig pen. "Oh, sweetheart! They are just the right size. Let's go pick one out."

As they looked at the variety of guinea pigs that they had to choose from, Anna said, “I want that cute little one in the corner.” The little guinea pig looked up in total astonishment and blurted, “Oh my! Did she just point at me?”

“I’m so happy.”

As soon as they arrived home, they put the little guinea pig into his cage. “So what are you going to name your new little friend?” asked Anna’s mother. “I don’t know, but it has to be something cute,” said Anna. “I think I’ll call him...”

“What do you want your name to be?” She asked her little guinea pig, than without waiting for an answer, Anna exclaimed. “That’s it. I shall name you Puddles.”

Puddles stared back at Anna with a loving smile and said to himself, "I think I am going to like it here."

Puddles and Anna became the best of friends, and they were never lonely anymore.

This Children's story was based on the real life story of our pet guinea pig, Puddles.

THE
END

TRACE AND COLOR

Trace and color the other halves of the pictures.
Then, trace the words.

HELP PUDDLES FIND HIS WAY

Help Puddles find his way through the maze. How many veggies can Puddles put in his veggie bowl, following the right path?

Number of veggies	

FIND THE LETTERS.

DIRECTIONS: PUDDLES STARTS WITH THE LETTER P.
TRACE THE LETTERS. THEN COLOR THE CIRCLES THAT HAVE THE LETTER P.

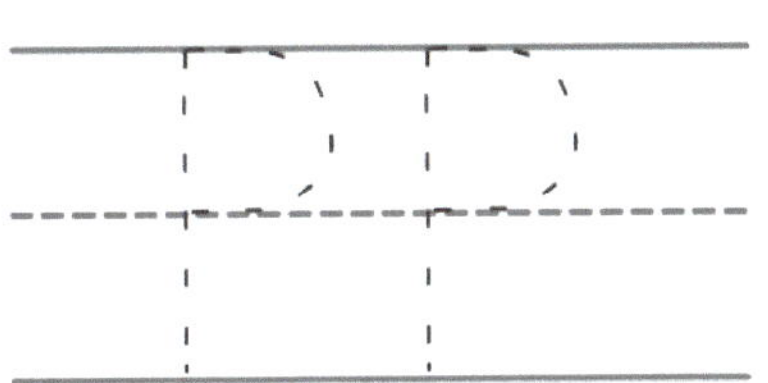

is for Puddles

VEGGIE COUNT

Puddles loves veggies! Help him count the veggies and write the correct number

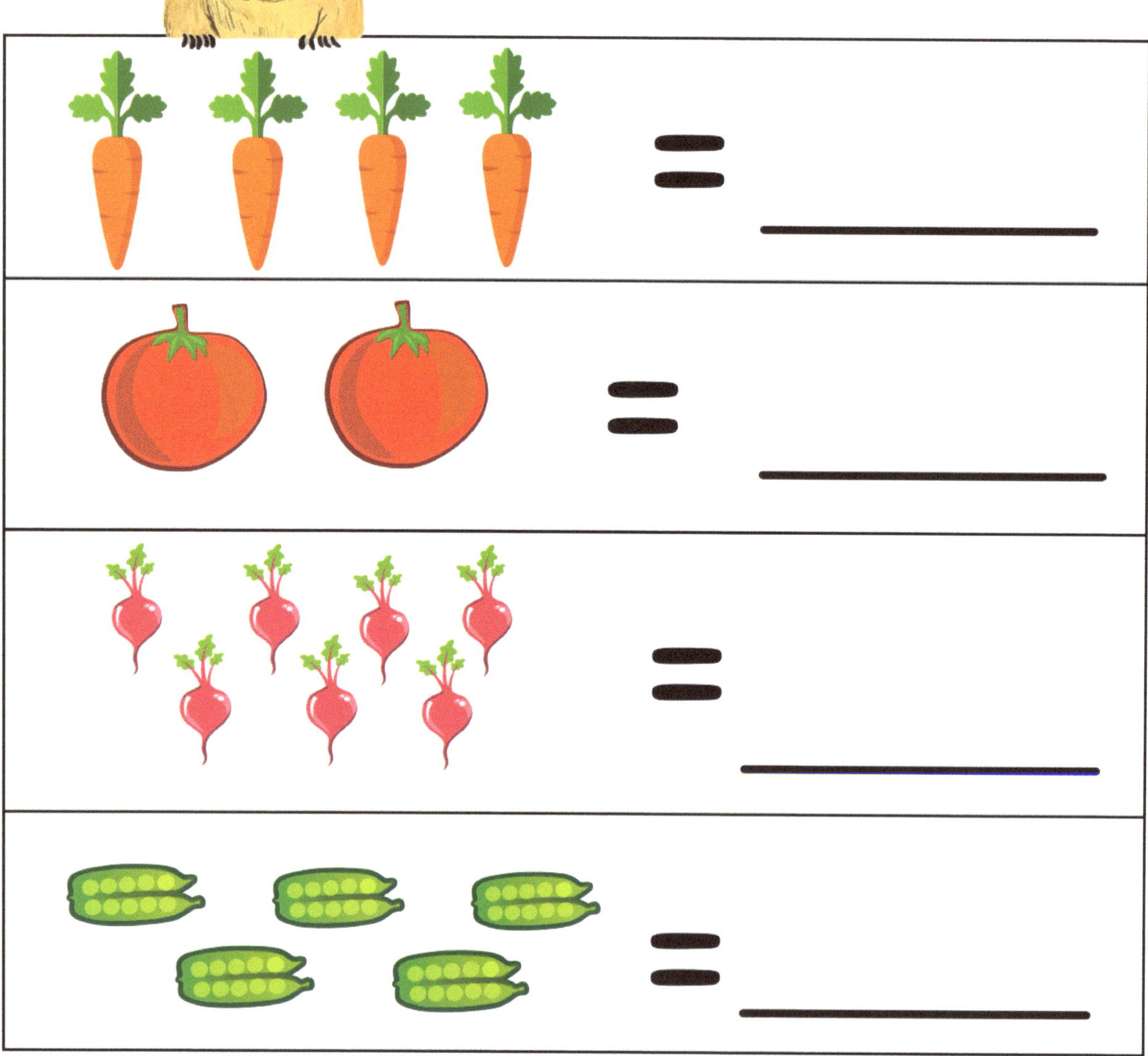

DO YOU KNOW YOUR ALPHABET

Help Puddles and Anna fill in the missing letters

A C E

G H

J K L N

Q R T

V X Z

Snack Time!

Look at the pictures below and select five healthy snacks for Puddles.

WORD SEARCH

Help Puddles find the words below!

h	s	g	h	t	u	t	d	c	l	s	g	y	l	a
a	l	d	n	e	g	o	a	x	a	n	n	a	d	v
y	l	y	c	i	a	e	g	v	l	u	i	p	n	e
x	i	s	o	d	i	r	u	i	p	t	d	o	g	g
m	k	s	u	h	f	r	i	u	t	t	e	b	u	e
m	s	q	u	e	a	k	n	n	y	e	e	n	a	t
g	l	m	l	k	b	m	e	w	g	r	f	s	g	a
x	a	r	t	i	c	u	a	a	t	i	o	o	e	b
i	i	s	w	a	l	l	p	w	i	n	g	c	e	l
y	c	a	r	e	t	i	l	h	f	h	p	i	c	e
d	o	h	i	r	d	e	g	o	y	r	p	a	i	s
p	e	t	s	t	o	r	e	m	v	x	i	l	o	i
s	p	s	h	j	f	s	d	e	q	e	v	e	v	n
s	l	p	q	w	o	t	i	a	c	x	d	n	n	s
t	l	m	k	a	w	a	d	o	p	t	i	o	n	d

ANNA
HAY
GUINEA PIG
ADOPTION
VEGETABLES
PET STORE
FRIEND
SQUEAK
HOME
LOVE
FRUIT
SOCIAL

DRAW A PICTURE OF A

NEW FRIEND FOR PUDDLES?

Puddles loves to make new friends. Can you draw a picture of a new friend for Puddles? What would they look like?

www.ingramcontent.com/pod-product-compliance
Ingram Content Group UK Ltd.
Pitfield, Milton Keynes, MK11 3LW, UK
UKHW060114300726
14090UKWH00002B/194

* 9 7 8 1 0 8 8 0 4 5 8 5 5 *